eighteen

alberto ramos

eighteen

lived written and illustrated by

alberto ramos

ISBN: 978-1-7292-5629-9

to sofie liljestrand

contents

preface

eighteen is a journey of growth and becoming
it is divided into three parts

the ending deals with abuse and homophobia
bullying and suicide
loss and trauma

the transition explores self-discovery
healing and grieving
life and death
forgiveness and moving on

the beginning is a celebration of one self
of the existing beauty in this world
it exudes self-love and power
joy and hope after the sorrow

love and grief are the only themes present in every part

this whole reflection of experiences is meant to
immerse you with me into the eyewall of the hurricane
after it is over i hope it helps you realize things are
usually more complex than they seem
and despite the darkness surrounding you
a new beginning is always possible
as long as you are willing to welcome it

letter to you

regardless of what hands this book reaches
i hope it makes yours stronger

i hope it helps you understand in case you are
going through a hardship that life are stages

that helps you realizing how complete you are
how strong you can be
how much power you carry within

i hope what you are about to experience
inspires you provokes you
moves you touches you

i hope you enjoy the journey
that it makes you feel
but above all

i hope it makes you think

                                        yours truly

                                        Alberto Ramos

the ending

i know you don't want to see this
but you must open yourselves
i tell my eyes

life is going to proceed anyway
it's not going to wait for us just
cause we want her to
no answer

we can't be having this conversation
every morning

i feel the salt of the first tear
sliding its way down my cheek

this is how i know the day started

— the ending

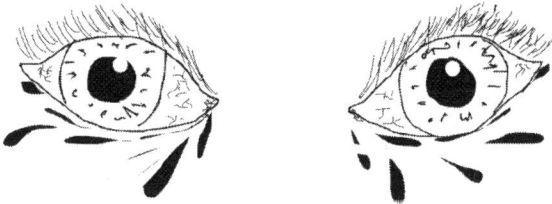

eighteen years ago
i was born in the furthest part of myself

listening to my weepy ears
saddened and frustrated
cause they heard how awful it is to be me
my eyes have rolled themselves out
to unsee
what they had seen the world was making
out of me
my mouth has grown silent
scared of pronouncing herself
for craving what she was taught to reject

from the first breath the world placed
a curse on me and i am yet undoing it

tell me how
could i not begin
with endings and
end with beginnings

these young legs
are sore
from the grief
of getting on their knees
not to pray
but for other things
a child
should never be
manipulated
to do

— after church

i could pour entire oceans in your lips
and that wouldn't satiate
the thirst
of your culpability

— *when you ask me to do as if it never happened*

i must admit i have
been scared at the chance
what he teared off
from me it's
never
coming back but
what really terrifies me is
if it does come back
and i can no longer
recognize it

— conversations with my body
(the aftermath)

every time
you fooled my heart
my body knew

my soul still aches
from the first time he touched me

— *butterfly effect*

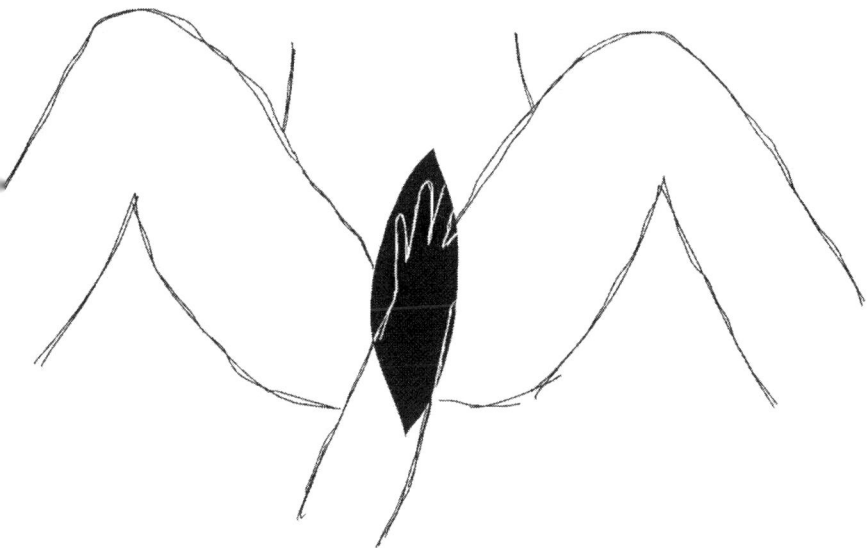

on days like this
the alarm that wakes me up
are the shouts of my body

the memory of you
clings to my hips
every night as if
it happened yesterday

— mo(u)rning

to keep your warmth
in a place that tries so hard
to turn you cold

— the challenge

they will make you think it is your fault that they hurt
you. cutting you in half and putting the knife in your
hands afterwards. they like power and control. they
think they are somehow above you. that you are
defenseless. and they try to make you believe it too.
they assume they win over you. they don't know what
genuine empathy is despite fooling themselves into
believing they do. they destroy and harm.
and you will not see them holding genuine
accountability for their actions.

but despite pages and pages could be written about how
they make you feel. the pain they provoke. the wounds
they put salt on just to make the healing more hurtful.
the way they seem to always pretend they are alien to
the problem they caused. and how they crush you when
you were drowning and all you needed was a helping
hand. one word is enough to describe them.
fear.

— *abusers*

my mind couldn't teach
my body how
to pretend
nothing had happened when
everything was happening

i guess what can't think
can't fool itself

— abuse

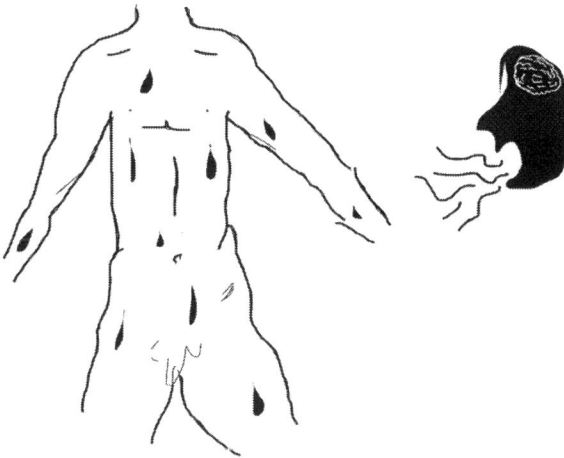

i am a firm believer pain
can show you the way but
i also believe one may not be
ready to digest all the pain
just to see the way

i am always doubting
whether i should
save the world
or save me from it

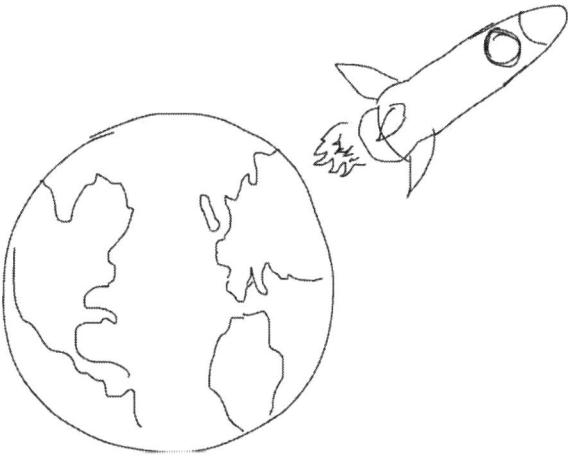

spit on me
hit me
insult me
harass me
hate on me
tell them you don't know me
that you don't hang with creeps
manipulate their perception of me
make me look like a beast
like a freak
wish my death

but
just don't be surprised
if long after i'm gone
i appear in the middle of the night
as a heavy presence
on your soul
and tear it in half

— *guilt*

i became fond of
the monster
under my bed
and now i fear he leaves

you point out
the way to hell for me
as they taught you that is
where i belong
cause my lips were born hungry
for the taste of other men

and i wonder
do you really think
someone who speaks and
justifies hatred
in the name of another
they don't even know
is worth of your trust

— *teacher*

telling your parents
that you're scared for your life
when going to school cause
the students want you dead

— homework

i had to
survive in
waters
i never swam
in
before.

how could i not be different.

— *metamorphosis*

bullying feels
like drowning in a tsunami
from a sea of microscopic minds
struggling to keep
the last breath of reason

— to be sane in insane places

i danced along the melody of your lies
for so long i can no longer
tune in with my own
symphony

to be hidden is
one of the worst
cruelest thing
that can be done to a human being

— you don't hide what you're proud of

to be invisible
to be surrounded by
people who don't want
your light
to shine brighter than theirs
it's not about not being
the first option but
rather not being an option at all
to be invisible
to be surrounded by selfishness

— *don't let them dictate your value*
  (nobody is alien to envy)

in time it started to make sense
the kids i had seen on tv
taking their lives away
out of sorrow
i felt for a moment
connected to them
as if we were stars shining
under the same constellation
i couldn't see them
and they couldn't see me
but we felt each other so
intensely as if
we had been one
in other lifetimes

i wondered if i'd ever be
one of them

— self-destruction

you left me wondering
who gave you the brush and paints
to deliverately draw sorrow
in this face.
what made you feel powerful enough
to persecute me.
does it give satisfaction to you.
do you prove something to yourself
by trying to run over me.
to crush me like an insect.

you go after the ones you can tell
have no weapons
to fight you and your crew
as if.
you were waiting for a surprise
as if.
when you tear me
in half
something comes out of me as a prize.

— questions

he tells the kids
i should be
burning in hell
instead of studying at school.
he gives them entitlement.
to bury alive
what deviates from the standard.
he enmasks his hatred as
love and faith and
talks in the name of
somebody
who would find him despicable.
he.
tells them my lungs are not
worthy
of the air they breathe
cause he claims he read it in a book.

— *answers*

asking me to avoid some topics
cause they are controversial
is asking me to avoid myself—
even if i wanted to. i cannot.
i am a gay man.
my way of talking. dressing. being.
are vexed.
my relationships
are open to discussion.
every move i make
is harshly judged.
my existence
is a hard pill to swallow.
i know as a fact
i was born and will die
in controversy and
hated—
and i will still remain controversial.

— *a happy controversy*

i live for the day when
people like me
everywhere
aren't afraid of
kissing their lover
in front of
the busiest station

— illegal love

real lgbtq stories – #mequeer

listening to your loved ones curse what you secretly are.

to get stolen the opportunity of the first teen love.

getting used to hear homophobic comments from your family towards openly gay public figures to later act surprised that you never had enough trust to come out of the closet to them.

fighting to find yourself for years in a society that claims you aren't worthy as you are. everything at the cost of your own mental health to later hear comments from your surroundings like *this is very hard for us to accept. you have to understand.*

to be forced by your parents or tutors to come out to them as gay disregarding that you're not ready just because they think that will help. absolutely ignoring what you feel.

having to search for lgbtq content on youtube to understand yourself cause you can't find characters nor references on series and movies for you to feel identified with.

that your partner passes away and you can't assist the funeral cause for their family. practitioners of god's assembly. you're the devil and an undesirable who perverted their child.

telling somebody that you're gay and that they try to flatter you by telling you *it's not noticeable*.

to feel anxiety when meeting new people in case they reject you again.

to get your life stolen.

to grow up listening to comments such as *do not cross your legs. do not dance like that. save those hands and do not make such gestures. you play too much with those dolls. you will never have a decent job.*

being unable to express affection publicly with your partner in case a crackpot feels like beating you up.

to be told that not beating you up is respecting you and that you should give that respect back by not showing your gayness.

to be considered a nobody by your partner's family despite being in a healthy relationship for years.

to be insulted and humilliated out of the blue in your daily life. having caused no harm to nobody.

to be told by your parents to hide. and. if you don't and they beat you up. you deserve it.

to feel you'll never be liked nor even by yourself.
to avoid talking in situations with strangers for them not to hear your voice and ridicule it.

for your sexual and sentimental life to start five to ten
years delayed.

having nobody to go to when you're breaking inside
cause your life is a secret nobody knows despite some
suspect. and worse is the fear of what they'll say if you
confess who you are than damaging your mental health.

that if we travel *little happen to us for what we seek.*
and if we don't we're *crying dramaqueens and we
should go to saudi arabia to see what they do with
people like us.*

to be provoked to commit suicide for being who you
are despite having caused no harm to nobody.

to be harassed at work and school where you're
supposed to go to work and learn.

having panick for school.

to be spat on for kissing your partner publicly.

to be peed on you by all your classmates on the locker
rooms cause according to them you looked too much
to one of them.

to be absolutely lost about who you are. not taken
serious by anybody. feeling there's something wrong
with you. having to explain all the time what you are.
to get your identity refused.

looking around before kissing somebody publicly.

to be rejected by your family. kicked out of your home. insulted. humilliated. to be told by them they wish you were dead.

to be told by your dad that your mother cries every night wondering what did she do wrong and that it's all your fault.

crying and praying for somebody to come change you. to cure you. cause you feel you are a freak. an abomination.

that family members call your partner *friend* cause your cousins are kids and *they don't understand it.*

to be told by your crying mother that she's scared you get killed or beaten up for being gay.

not having straight friends cause as soon as you show the slightest affection they get away cause *i respect you and all that but i'm not into that stuff.* that such different treatment leads you to have a chronical insecurity in further relationships with heterosexual men in any situation.

that everybody favorite moment at school. recess. becomes your worst nightmare.

to be shouted by policemen in a police car *time to sleep you faggots* when you're with your friends at the closing of a gay club.

to be afraid of holding your partner's hand.

to get your childhood stolen and to have no weapons to defend yourself.

to feel that your friends are ashamed of you in a way so sutile it looks like it's all in your head when you exteriorize it. although deep inside you both know it is true. to feel so terribly alone and misunderstood you call friends to such people.

to be scared of walking through the corridors of your school cause of the background laughs and comments towards your way of walking. talking. dressing. being.

being unable to speak out on a sexual aggression experience cause besides the shame guilt and pain it provokes itself you have to add the intern debate with your sexuality making it way more difficult and painful.

to feel you'll never find love as a teen cause gays are better hidden than waldo.

to feel forced to like people you don't like cause *that's what you get. on top of being gay you can't be demanding.*

not being allowed to hold your cousins and little siblings after coming out as gay cause your mother thinks since you like men you like children too.

these stories come from souls so different
the only thing they've in common is not being
what they were told they should
this is the fight that unite us
this is the blood of millions of lgbtq people

cause homosexuality isn't normalized
but homophobia is

this is for you to understand why gay pride is essential
and why it's crucial to give extra special attention
to things such as *little* discriminatory comments
you don't need to belong to this collective
you only have to show humanity
to practice empathy
try to understand what others feel
don't think of yourself as the exception
that what you do causes no harm to nobody
that they understand what you mean
that you're just like that

micro-homophobia is worse than extreme homophobia
when it's multiplied by a hundred
and it isn't a matter of freedom of speech
homophobia kills
and ignorance has the blood in its hands

i've been forced to undergo some tests
in order to cure my homosexuality—
doctor lopez ibor practised me a lobotomy
according to him it was a success
but the truth is it has caused me difficulties
to move and talk

— *medicine victim in europe 1973*

i should have known
i can't trust a world
where a part of its people
demand the killing of
another part
for expressing love while
a third part watches
doing nothing about it

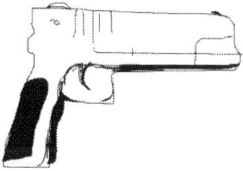

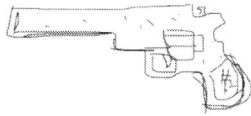

it was us who made
something admirable
out of cruelty
turning
carelessness and coldness
instead of kindness and empathy
into desirable traits
we're trapped in ignorance cause
our mentors are instructing us
into not learning

— *education*

resilience
is power

when fighting isn't an option
resist

you will be what you do
the challenges you dared to take
the things you eventually did say
the actions you didn't just think of doing
but the ones you carried out

and not what is left unsaid
what had the potential of becoming
what could have been
what you thought could be a good idea
and did nothing about

— at the end

how can i escape if
i think i'm free already
i need to comprehend i'm trapped
before i run for freedom

they say *you shouldn't be afraid*
of being who you are
yet my entire soul shakes
everytime i attempt to be
that *you shouldn't teach them*
to respect you
they should know
you deserve respect too
yet i crave that respect so much
when i get it i mistake it for love

sometimes i like to imagine
how different my life would be
if things had been how they
should
since the very beginning

— *what should be and what is*

i am so tired
of being used like a kleenex
i am not a disposable thing
for you to use whenever you are
in need of saving yourself

— i have my own scars to take care of

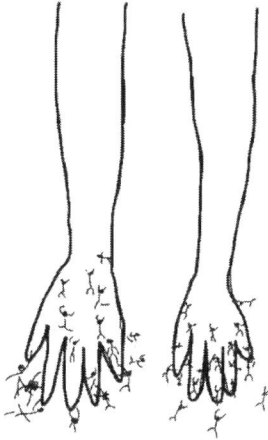

you can love me the most
your way
yet have no idea how to
make me feel loved
my way

if you need glasses to see
my most open wounds
to see the real me
comprehend how i feel
what i need
how to please me
what moves me
what makes me tender
if despite how bad you try
you don't understand
the light in me
that is when
love is
not
enough

— *translation*

i am insulting
the person i am by
trying to be
a person i'm not
causing eczema
on this canvas
my body is
by drawing
with cheap paints

— self-harm

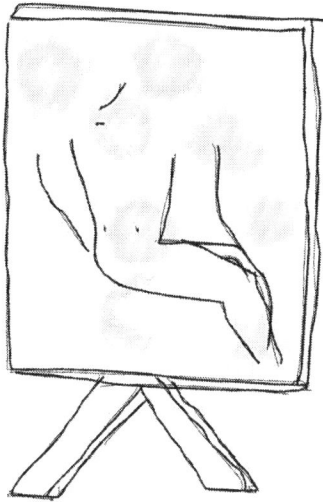

you made love look
so complicated i wonder
if craving it
from those
incapable of loving me
is a punishment or
a blessing

you are like skipping diet
eating too much chocolate
going on a shopping spree
spending too much
thinking too little
i know i shouldn't
yet i do you

— *guilty pleasure*

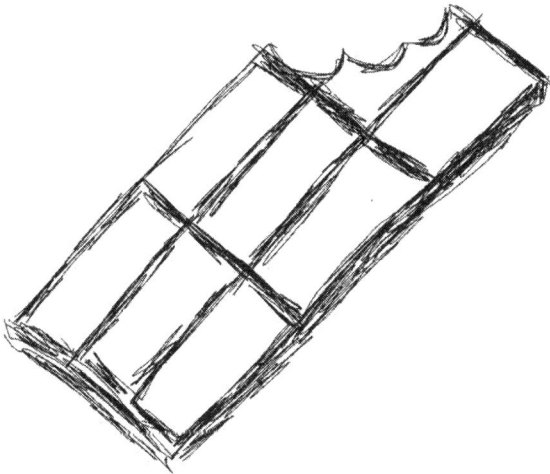

absence will grab your hand
and test you
pushing you away from
everything you love
company is at heart
she says
before she leaves

— *loss will show you the way or*
  make you hold the wrong hands

i want to build my house in your arms

— home is
where your hands are

there is nothing sexier
than the smell of logic
dripping off
my wrists

— *fragrance*

it was the spine of
your back
who
begged me
to stay

— don't be mistaken

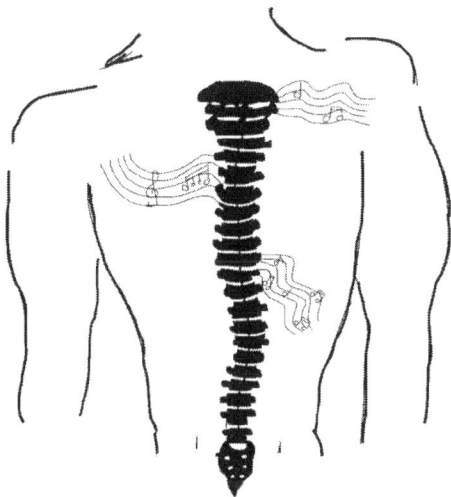

your company
felt like living
in
all the places i love
at once

your absence
left me homeless

— *moving out*

i became fire
just to be your light

i am growing up
thinking i am my only
company cause those
who are like me
are hidden

— *representation*

they say not knowing
where you're going
may lead you to
your least favorite destinations

— us

i am tired of waking up feeling
insufficient

worse than
          lesser than
                    uglier than

as if i had to compete
to perfectionate myself
to prove something to
this world
to the people who don't even
acknowledge
my existence

— the search

do not come here
looking for full-time rationality
just like you—
i am a constant contradiction

you were blind towards
what you chose not to see
i guess darkness is
too temptress for those
who are scared of the light

.

~~the truth is i have been finding more home in the lips of~~
~~strangers than in entire mouths of acquaintances. that~~
~~nothing is nor will ever be the same and everyday~~
~~pushes me more far away from myself.~~
~~that i lowkey want it to be that way. and i feel forced to~~
~~pretend i do not. to act and fake.~~
~~the truth is i started to believe the people who kept~~
~~saying my existence is wrong and i interiorized it.~~
~~i swear i did not want to. or at least so i think.~~
~~but now it's dark and raining and the only sound of my~~
~~voice triggers pain in my most inner being.~~
~~my relationship with myself has been a punishment and~~
~~loving anything makes it difficult to love myself. the~~
~~truth is my heart speaks more clear when i'm away.~~
~~from myself. that my breath is finally at peace when i~~
~~leave and my absence comes.~~
~~i am terrified at the thought of myself.~~
~~i am lost within my surroundings and a part of me does~~
~~not want find its way back.~~
but who cares about the truth.

the truth will open your soul
and tear it off your chest
but
you can
survive it

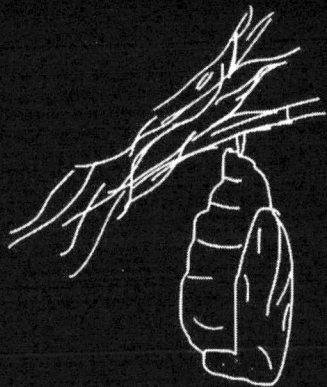

the transition

a transition
takes becoming
healing
letters
pain
time
willingness

but above all
a transition
takes honesty

— the transition

pretending you are defending somebody. acting up as if you were doing everything in your power to make a change. to support a cause. to help. is by no means the same as actually doing it. cause we can all make up excuses to justify our mistakes giving away our blame to others. but you should know. that when a situation is so unbalanced that it is hundreds of individuals against one individual. that one individual needs at the very least. loyalty. that if somebody supports them. for it to be genuine. for that person to be willing. to hold this weight when the soul waives and it falls to the floor. someone that will back them up with no excuses. a bit of humanity. and not your sham support or false words. which only make the sinking worse.

you saw me split myself open to you so that you could see my soul was tearing. only to be left opened in half. did you think something would happen out of nowhere. or that symphatizing with the bully would be the answer. did you really think this was an equal situation. or that i would not have something better to do than falling apart at your office making up fictious scenarios. do you think i am a number. cause you went back home to your life treating me as if i was. as if it was not due to you to make a change in the school you work in. as if it was my fault that i got bullied. and the best that could happen would be for me to leave. so that you could put a fancy veil on what happened. covering up the crime scene with words as full of love as they are of lies. tell me. is it my life that is worth so little. or is it your ego that's made of gold.

meanwhile. i thought of dropping school and ending my precious life. tell me. would it had been easier. if i had finished the destruction work the students had already started on me. so that you could freely pretend you did everything in your power to keep me alive. what would i have become. please tell me. would you have made postcards in remembrance. of the unfortunate boy who could not stand it anymore. would you have sent flowers to my family. would you have made a talk for the students to let them know how much you supported me. how sad it is i am gone.

if i'm alive today. if i can tell my story. it is not because of you. it is cause i've grown thick skin and have a real support base that backed me up with warmth so full of love i managed to light up the whole city. i guess you could even look me in the eye. as my soul tears. and say you did everything you could to avoid the massive destruction your students were making out of me. cause lies is the language you're most fluent in.

my life is not a simulation to be repeated. i am to be treated like a human. not a number. i don't give a damn about your rules and regulations. i could be dead if it was up to those. so next time somebody seeks help in you. help them. or do not. and find somebody capable of providing help. but do not pretend you do offer help when you do not. cause if i was dead today. my blood would not only be in the hands of the ones who tried to reduce my existence to ashes. it would be in yours too.

— letter to you who could've helped this but didn't

you disguise as hope and i am the guilt
we both come
and go from our minds at midnight.

— *mirror*

you may have not provoked
the fire i burned in
but what you did
was to provide the
materials
situations and
circumstances
for the fire to be given
all just to stand there still
contemplating how
i
flew up in flames

— when you tell me it's not your fault

i should never be told
i must leave somewhere else
if i want to be respected
as if respect is something
i have to earn
as if i had to pass a test
to get to be respected
and i had already failed
before exiting my mother's belly
you think it's fair
that i didn't get the chance to be
anything else rather than
what you heard
people like me
are

and yet
you decide to play safe
not to look at me in the eye as i break
not to see me getting harassed everyday
and instead of helping me
you suggest me to go seek respect
somewhere else

— when the counselor suggests other schools
would be a better option for people like me

playtime is over
cause i no longer want to be appealing
i want to be me
i have not made this long journey
to be anybody's prey
i won't change to please you
to adapt to your necessities and wishes
pretending to be something i'm not
to fit into your expectations of me
of what i could potentially be
according to you

i am what i am
take it or leave it

— letter to society

there's so much to be thankful for in this life.
respect is nonetheless never. ever.
one of those things.

be thankful for those who hold your heart in their naked
hands. and protect it. as if it was theirs. notice the one
who becomes the sun when your life is a dark storm.
regardless living at a dark storm themselves. whenever
they're a broken light for you. just to warm you up.
whenever they do anything for you. for the sake of
loving you. appreciate the one who takes the darkness
in you and kiss it all the way till its root. don't take a
genuine love for granted. show you gratitude and
appreciation. everytime. cause we all like to feel that
our efforts. the light. invested in what we do.
is appreciated.
to feel seen.

— *hypermetropia*

i remember your eyes boiling
in anger
because of seeing
a reflection
of what you'd like to be
and are not

— free

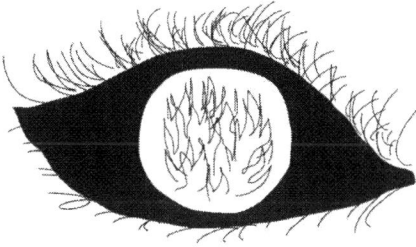

do not turn into a threat
with your manipulative attitude
when i stand up for myself
when i don't say
but show
who i am
what i am made of
what i am capable of
cause it isn't a threat
it's a statement

you can't just come here
to erase my limits and
build your own
all over my body

treating me like a ragdoll
and coming back at my feet
while i am yet shattered
picking up the pieces of myself left
after your mistakes
helplessly rubbing all of your *sorry's*
on my skin to help it heal
one day a wrecking ball
the next day a little lamb
healing doesn't work like that

your acting
of regret is if anything
entertaining
expecting that's enough for
me to pretend
nothing has happened
is if anything
naive

isn't it sad and funny
the fact that some people really act as if being kind
can make up for the fact that they treat you poorly
and have no genuine appreciation
respect
nor kindness of any type towards you
like if when they have the power to do something that
would make life easier for you yet decide not to do it
that's going to be compensated by empty kindness
let me tell you something
for me
kindness comes from deep within
for me kindness is wishing one well
vibrating good energy to one another
if your kindness was genuine
it wouldn't depend on a third cause
you are kind because of
to your type of kindness i call pretending
if you somehow invoke mixed feelings
—distrust one of them
everytime you are kind
you're not really kind
you're just manipulative

— to what you call kindness i call manipulation

you often don't get to choose
what you go through
the role you're put in
what you can do is
to shine through it

— your inability to see my light
doesn't mean i'm not shining

you can't know
till you embody the
shame in your skin
how much courage
it takes to
stand up
to show and be proud
of who you are
in a world that taught
you to become
the silence

hold yourself tight
every night before sleeping
be happy
you will always got you

it does help

— self-love is built everyday

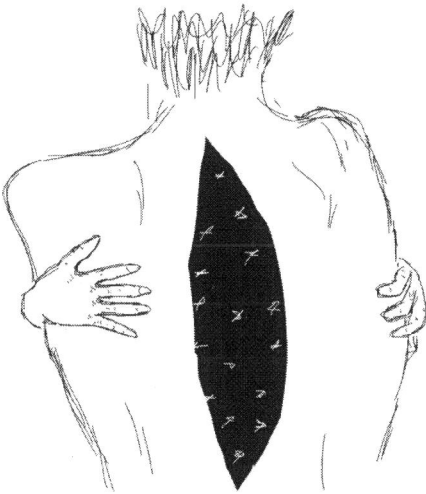

you say we live in an open place. that we are free
people. my dear. who is it you're trying to fool. with 77
countries to date where homosexuality is a punishable
activity. where they define our love as sodomy. mental
disorder. unnatural. anti morality. promoting sexual
deviancy. among others.

how are we going forward. if when people move they
take their beliefs with them as a precious treasure
wherever they go. and these days people are moving
more than ever. and by no means we should stop
moving. in fact moving is the most beautiful thing that
can happen to many. but. for our journeys to be safe.
and for our souls to be treated carefully. there should be
way more real protection towards minorities like lgbtq
when for instance people with homophobic beliefs
move to non-homophobic countries.

the law should be adapted to this situation of constant
movement and growth life is for everybody to be safe.
my own skin knows persecution to gay people occurs in
stockholm sweden as recently as 2018 and there are no
real consequences towards those abusing. despite them
being reported to police. this isn't what freedom to
move should mean. why. somebody trying to have a
peaceful journey. cannot. because of the little concern
and action taken to protect their right to be.

ask yourself before hosting anybody whether you can
guarantee the safety to freely be. whatever we are or
want to be. gay. black. trans. or anything. with no fear
of persecution. and if the answer is yes. welcome them.
if not. but they need to be hosted. educate them and

protect the people living here to freely be who they're.
everybody deserves the chance to a decent life but not
at the cost of making other's existence miserable.

and then. the fact that in most western countries we are
not being exposed to major state violence nor that our
sexual orientation is not considered a mental disorder or
crime does not mean that we have equal rights either.
nor that we receive equal respect. cause we do not. it is
about time to change this. we're so sick of the *no homo*.
of the passive-aggressive attitude. or the assumption
that we're going to be attracted to every man on this
earth just for being gay. is it really that bad for a straight
guy to be seen or portrayed as gay. tell me. do you
become a monster. an undesirable freak. we're so tired
of being the lesser. the ones that need to try the hardest
to be *accepted*. to be respected.

it is pathetic. after all this time of so-called evolution.
having to say this. stop ridiculing anything with a gay
connotation. it doesn't make you any cooler. plus what
you think of as an innocent comment adds up to a huge
pile. you're not the only one who thought that way. stop
acting as if we should show gratitude towards your
respect. your acceptance. we will never be thankful that
our existence is respected. we are human beings. and so
are you.

— letter to sweden | to the world

my blood clings to your hands
from these pages
and you aren't even noticing

perhaps it was my ambition
or that i lived with a blindfold
not wanting to acknowledge
what my eyes saw
my circunstancial role
perhaps the inner-me
refusing to accept
having come this far to
only come this far
or this cold city that
clouded my ideas so that
i ended up unable to think clear
maybe it's stockholm syndrome

— why i stayed

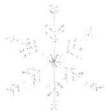

do not betray the country that hosted you.
its people and its law
just because it's not the same
as the one you come from.
just because it does not follow your customs.
this country is hugging you
and you are bitting it in return.
calling whores to the girls who
pass by the streets of their homeland
cause they don't wear what
you were taught they should.
cursing and beating up
homosexual people
just cause you would
stone them to death
in your country.
this is a new chapter for you and
we are offering our helping hand
for this journey to be a soft one
don't spit in it.

— *adaptability*

the glimpse of warmth
that keeps me
soft
inside the storm
i owe to
myself

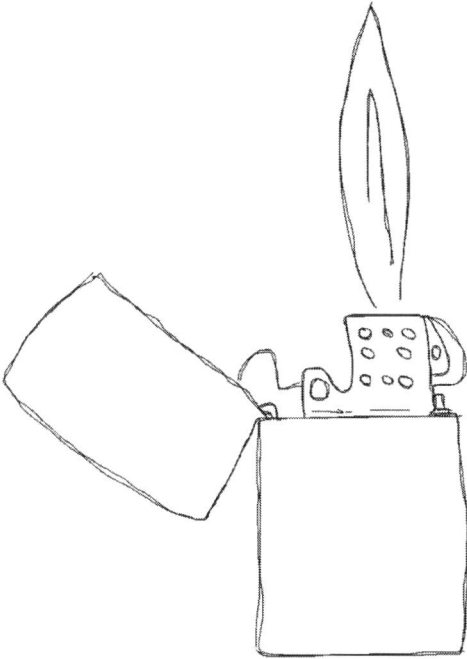

the desire to see you hurting
is the only thing shining in their empty faces
you can tell from miles away
they crave your suffering
your pain. your death.

but don't be scared—
this is the side effect of glowing

seeing you dead would mean
not having to see someone who
gets along with their breath
while their bitter soul
is eating alive their organs one by one
and forcing them to watch

— one day you'll regret all the bad you wished me

i assume the blame
for losing my balance
and holding just anyone's hand

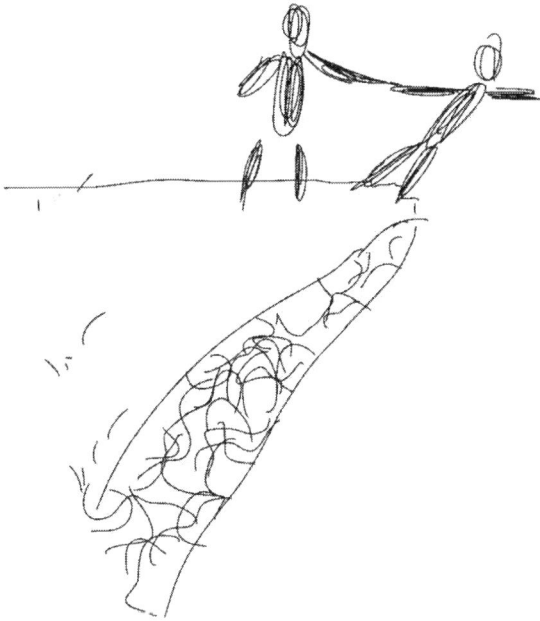

these waters remind me that regardless of how small the world may seem sometimes. when you genuinely believe everyone. and everything. is picking on you. for whatever reason. they really are nothing. nobody. nor anything. is relevant enough to make you feel less than a whole. there's always something else. somebody willing to love you for each person willing to hate you. this world is immense. and full of people willing to appreciate your light just as it is. to cheerish you just as you are. split yourself open to the world. enjoy the little things. each breath. travel. love. surround yourself with people that inspire you. but above all. fall in love with who you are.

— *things långsjön taught me*

i admire the people who grew up listening to rubbish yet decided to ignore it. and educate themselves. given that the brains of the ones supposed to do so were on vacation. having the courage to acknowledge that the figure that is supposed to teach them. the so called role model. an older age or more *relevant* position. does not necessarily mean being right.

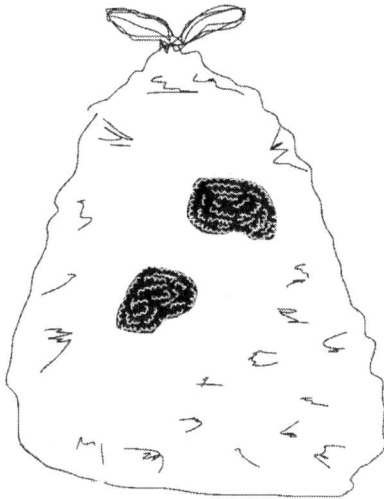

me believing in softness.
kindness.
and peace.
does not translate
into empowering
you.
to deliverately
hurt.
disrespect.
and mistreat
me.

— *i snap back*

i often ask myself
why
do i keep on expecting
love
from those who have clearly shown
disinterest

i know you were taught this is a dangerous world and craziness is all over the place but. my love. if you. the person i trust most to kiss my wings and believe in my potential tackles me to the floor tell me what we do. sometimes we have to risk. walk on the edge of the cliff so that we get to feel the breeze. run through the wild so that we get to hear the birds singing along and we can dance to their melodies. sometimes we have to give it all. for what we love. for ourselves. one should never be too afraid of living cause the price of being so is already the highest unimaginable—losing your life.

you may not change this cruel world
but what you do is
to make my stay here
feel like paradise

— *your essence*

i love
the sound of
my voice when i speak
for you

what can i do when
you say my name and
i become music

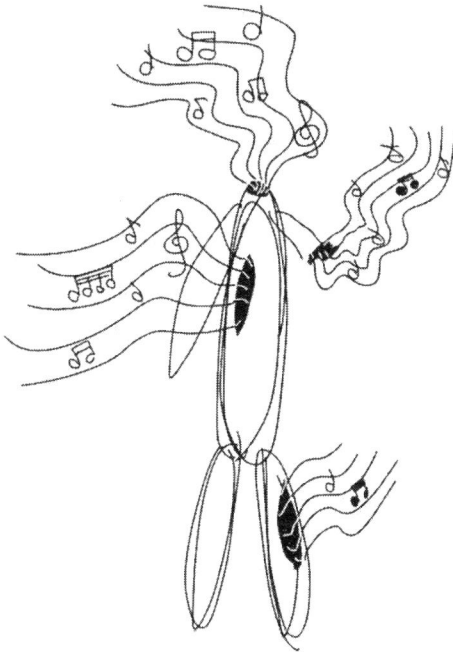

despite our eyes seem to see
opposite worlds
we can't help fall in love
with our looks
we are proof
that just thinking different
doesn't have to drift us apart
the willingness of understanding
each other
instead of judging
keep us together

but if it does eventually drift us apart
we'll prove then
no one dies of solitude
cause all i
need
is me

— *what love looks like*

i don't know whom
writes more
of the two of us
if i put the words
and you give them
meaning

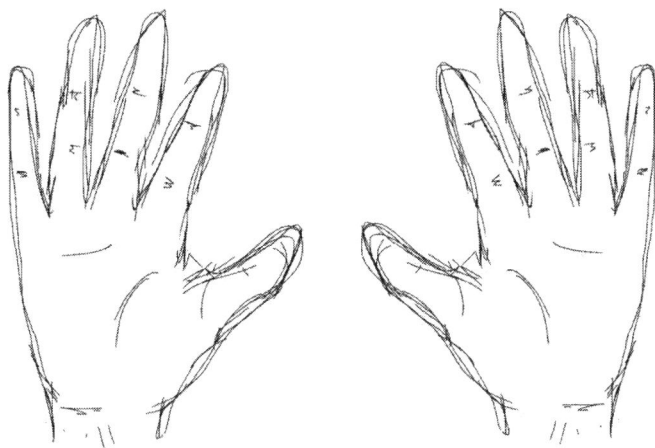

how could you learn to love if
you were raised by hatred

where did your light come from
if you were taught you
were the darkest place

— *within*

i'll give to the wind
the kisses i had saved for you
hoping so
i reach you

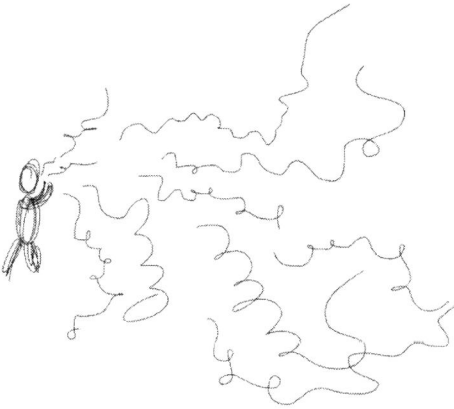

if only
i forgave myself
as easily as i've
forgiven you

i won't feel bad for not doing
what i don't want to do for you
just because you would do it for me
there is nothing more beautiful
than us being distinct and showing
love differently

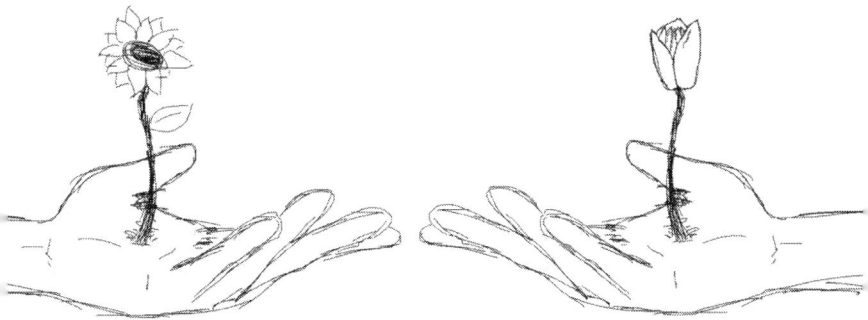

the line is
getting crossed
the very moment
you begin to feel like
you have a say in
how.
when.
what.
parts of my body
i show.

— *boundary*

i want our love to be
as strong as thin is
the line with the potential
to break it

— limits

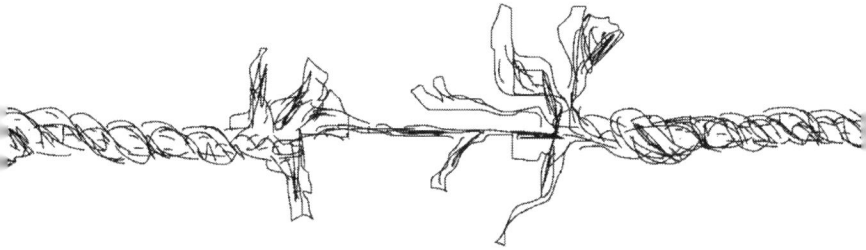

there's been too many times already. too many ways.
in which i have tried to approach you. the outcome has
always been the same. a waste of time. you have been
the audience to the fiction play i made out of our
relationship. where i constantly fooled myself into
believing you. cause trust me. i wanted to believe you.

everytime i attempted to love myself. you would make
a game out of my love. distort it. play the victim. and
leave me feeling as if loving myself was problematic.
as if i should do it in silence or straightforward not do
it. you have offered me abuse. toxicity. negativity.
harassment. disguised as love. cause that's *your way
of loving*. and i have been blind enough to eat it up.

but eventually. after swallowing lies deceits and sorrow
because of your selfishness. after being so full of it.
i am drowning. this dissapointment is way too great for
me to digest. and when i take a step back i notice. you'd
rather leave me drowning in pain by your side. just to
have me by your side. than to see me happy somewhere
else.

thank you for showing me what i do not want.

— *letter to my ~~lover~~ abuser*

my body liked to feel you
cause i told him to

my mind loved you
cause i taught her to

— *illusion*

abuse can disguise itself as sophistication
but it's still abuse

deceits
manipulation
emotional blackmail
taking advantage of situations
playing with sensitive information
and any other thing the abuser
may try to make you believe are
innocent and light-hearted
or simply in your head
are part of the abuse

— *you can't know if you have been abused*
   if you don't know what abuse is

there is a difference
between being available
and making myself
available
for you

i am learning
to forgive myself
for giving everything to those
who gave me nothing and
give nothing to those
who gave me everything

respect me enough to be authentic in my presence

everybody has the potential
to change
but not the willingness
save your precious time
and energy
by knowing whom
is whom

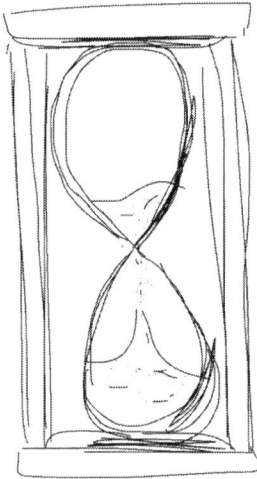

you tried to make a bargain out of me
by giving me the worst of you
in exchange of the best of me

— *your love and other forms of manipulation*

you are not unable to heal but
you are seeking cure
to your wounds
on the same tools
that provoked them

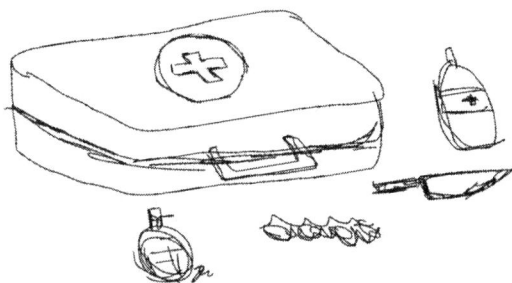

you tell me *you don't know what is like to be in this relationship* and yes. you are right. i don't know what is like to be in your relationship. but i can identify misery when i see it. i also know what it is like to get used to something. to assume a role and allow things. the *real* you. would never tolerate. and that we often blind ourselves towards what we rather not to see.

so don't build up walls. between yourself and the people who love you. and keep in mind your subjectivity. cause it is *your* relationship. is most likely. exactly. what makes your vision blurry so that you end up doing things. allowing things. the *real* you—that one we all know but you can't find anywhere—can't see.

what i hope you do see is that the very least thing those who love you utterly can do when we see your saddened heart is to intervene. cause you deserve to have by your side somebody who contributes to your growth. not a person who mistreats you and attempts to define your identity at their own ease.

remember you have one life to live. don't waste it besides someone who wants to own you. posses you. rather than to love you. i hope you find a light in your darkened path. hands to help you take away the veil that covered your eyes and didn't allow you to see it clear. to see the *real* you. you deserve peace in mind.

— letter to you surviving a relationship

you made me believe in
something that never existed
in the first place

love never expects
it wants you raw and free
happy and wild
longing on the other hand
is nothing but expectations

— *unaltered*

words and actions are
two different games
opposite at times
that not everybody knows
how to play

the more opposite your
words and actions are
the less
our game
will last

— *the balance*

blood doesn't tie me to anybody
i love the person who
sees
celebrates
respects
embraces and
loves
the light in me

— family

faith is a matter of believing
in hoping
in loving
in being
anything.
that is out of that.
is not faith.
is manipulation.

my body
is not meant to
be touched by
just anybody

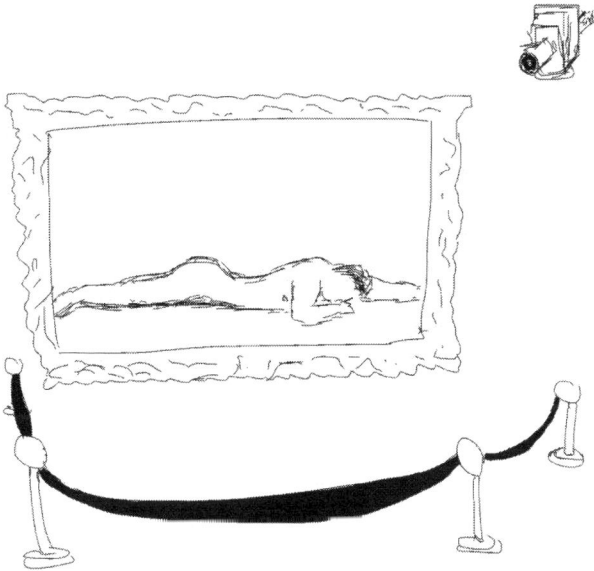

he pulls the moon down on my sheets
and the stars on my pillow.
this is how he puts my heart to sleep.

you will never seduce my mind with your body. cause
there is nothing that i admire more than comprehension.
open minds. empathy. and kindness. so don't give me
gifts. give me a part of your being. your time. your
essence. your thirst of knowledge. of experiences. of us.
i want to fall in love with the beauty of your mind.

if you want me to any extent. ask yourself. is your
exterior all you have to offer. because if so.
i'm not interested.

— my definition of beauty

how can you know if
you are unbreakable when
you've never been broken

— *strength comes after breaking*

do not hope
to be found
by them
they are not as tender
hope for you
to carry enough peace in mind
within that it
becomes so easy
to find yourself

— for you who finds beauty everywhere

let me be your family
take the spine of
my back and put it
in yours so
we share a bit of the great grief
your young soul carries
let me be your
home
to give you the love
you deserve
and this unfair world
takes away from
you
let me whisper to your
soul that you are
not alone
you never were
i see you
i have been you
and i love you

— letter to you. brave to love under a roof of hatred.

*if you feel like this weight is too much too handle.
call.* ***1-800-784-2433***

some people need not
to be home for
you to find home
within them

some people need not
to share blood for
you to find family
within them

— lost and found

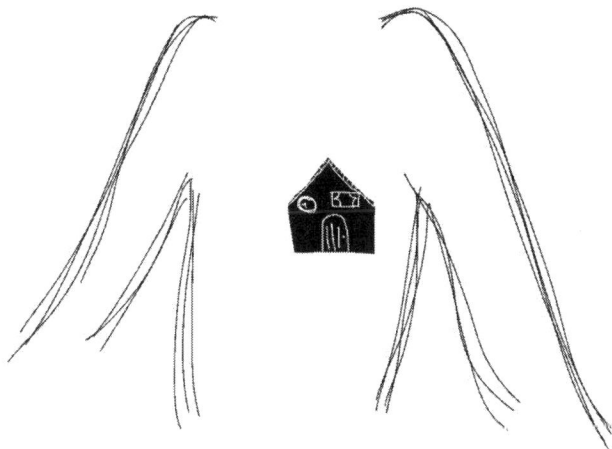

this brutal vulnerability
is your greatest tool
to heal
to love
to forgive
to move on
to shine

do not ever hide it

whenever grief lands
take off
to a more peaceful destination
make new decisions
hang with different people
feel different vibes

commit yourself
to land in a brighter place
than the one you came from

— move your roots

you will keep thinking they're irreplaceable
till you actually replace them

— *helpless*

life is a tale
and we are its characters
we don't come from one to hundred
afternight
growth is a process
a percentage
everyday in average if we work
smart enough
we get one per cent closer to the change
we plan on becoming
some days we may go back four per cent
others seven per cent forward

and one day
as if it happened all of a sudden
we will look back and realize
we're already there
at the brilliant long-awaited and glorious
hundred per cent

— marathon

a fierce getting bullied.
a strong feminine man.
a non-pitiful victim.
are valid.

you don't just become something
out of nowhere.
you are you.
before anything else
enters your life.
just because they are not used
to see something doesn't mean
that it is not valid.

don't let life happen to you
happen to her instead.
if you don't take your space
somebody else will.
if you let them dictate your value
they'll do so at their ease.

— *stereotype*

i don't want to feel embarrassed
of my body and its nature.
i don't want to feel strange
for being real.
i don't want to grow ashamed.
scared.
of a photograph.
i don't want to see this
as a competition.
i am enough the way i am.
i am so since the moment i was born.
why is everybody trying to make me think
otherwise.

these days we
are so focused on our answers
we forget others have questions too
we're blind to what doesn't interest us
but still choose to make such efforts
in causing a flawless impression
on people whose only thing we share in common
is our indifference towards one another
we yield to have the perfect smile
crave to get the impressing body
the perfect dimensions
when will we realize
we are already the full pack
enough and complete

— half

people who truly love you
should start to realize
what true love means
they should not be
pushing and pushing
and pushing
till you do what they think
is best for you
they should understand
a suggestion is enough
and celebrate your freedom
to choose whatever path you feel
will make you happier
without making you feel guilty for it
this is your life to live
not theirs

let your loved ones bloom

— letter to parents

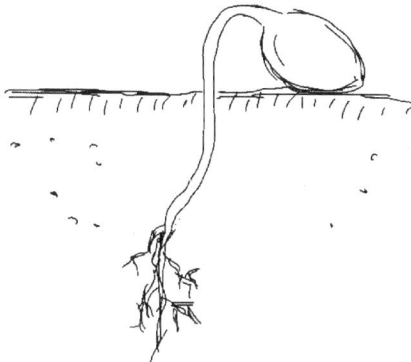

i know i like men
since i have
use of reason and
i don't need to try
out new things
nor to rethink about
my feelings
i am not not too young
nor too lost to
know what i like

or is it that only straight
children can know they are
straigh at a young age
without being questioned

— *not a phase*

leave mountains of distance with those who back off
when they see you are wilting cause they rather you to
bloom on your own and be back to them when you
already did instead of blooming with you.

— some people don't know what love is

money comes and goes
but time does not
so don't save anything
for later
words
trips
concerts
hugs
do it now
make time now
to do those things you enjoy
and bring joy to you
like birthdays do to kids
we come with no guarantees
for if we're not lucky
or life doesn't go too well
we're not playstations
neither we come with
second chances
life can't be restarted
or paused
it can only be lived
so make sure it is
a memorable one

— all we have is this moment

do not expect me to be
what you wish you had been yourself
i am not you and you are not me
i am not going to waste my life
letting you take decisions that
are meant to be taken by me
i love you more than words can express
but i have to draw my own lines
i have a life to live
decisions to take
mistakes to commit
and i can't let anybody do that for me
i am not a retrospective mirror
for you to look into your past
and rekindle it
to live through me
i can only hope for you to understand
to show enough maturity
cause i will not adapt
to something i was never born
to fit in

— letter to my creators

i might love you beyond love but
for the best
you will never be
my number one priority
that can only be
myself.

and if that is selfishness i am the most selfish.

— *letter to my loved ones*

with this many things to say
such many ways of doing so
and this many people to be reached
how could i stay quiet
sometimes we have so much
to say
to do
to see
to experience
we end up stressing out
drown in abundance
and do nothing

— get yourself together and start now

for what they have been exposed to. grown out of.
survived. created. and lived. women should be adored
and idealized. nevertheless. they aren't even fighting
for that. they simply ask for equity. what an insane
world we live in where this unequal treatment and
disadvantages exist towards the beings whose will
has been home to the miracle of life.

there is one thing we all have in common. women
made us. yet we're drowning them. pushing their
heads under water and asking them to breath. forcing
them into places so full emptiness and prejudices.
demanding them to become everything in silence.
putting blindfolds on their eyes and forcing them to
guide us. limiting them. and all just because there's
so much fear about them speaking up. having a voice.

do you know how it feels to. everyday.
get your needs ridiculed. to be catcalled. harassed.
objectified. not to be taken seriously. to get less for
doing the same job. to be body shamed.

to every whom ever dared disrespect a woman.
shame on you. respect your roots. all women are one.
remember the being you're shaming is the same one
that gave you life. you don't need to be a woman to
stand up for what's right. all you need is common sense.

we don't need to belong to the same category in every
aspect for us to protect each other. you don't have to be
a woman to notice unequity. you're already a human.
a being. that's what we all have in common.
stop marginalizing and separating. and start unifying.

so repeat after me. shout it loud.
a woman gave me breath
a voice to speak and these hands to feel
i won't use the blessings she honoured me with
as a weapon against her
again and again and again.
women bodies are miracles
to be admired and not molested
grab the nearest mirror and shout louder.
women are life
i am forever thankful as for a woman
i am alive.

— *i would be proud to be a woman*

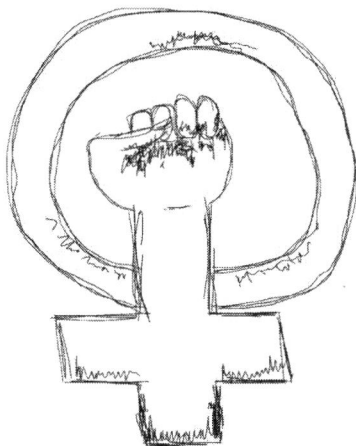

love the gift life is. unconditionally. and don't compare
yourself. your path. to others who have more. we all
belong to our own time and achieve things at a different
timing and with different skills. don't let simple-minded
people influence you. do not let them stop you. from
being who you are. every rarity that flows spontaneously
from you is a pure and gorgeous blessing to be
embraced. not to be ashamed of.

people will literally hate you for what you are and that
must not stop you from being so. as long as that is the
person you want to be. if otherwise. you can always
start again. to be a new you. as many times as you like.
don't ever let anyone get comfortable disturbing you.

— *human things*

show empathy. you are not the only person that struggles in this world. sometimes we're too focused on our own problems and dramas that we become fully blind to others. and we all have our own issues nor good nor bad. kindness is a precious gift which costs nothing. but if you choose not to be kind at least do not be the reason either why someone feels bad about themselves.

and whenever you realize something. anything. wrong you have done. acknowledge yourself for noticing and forgive yourself. it's indeed never too late to change. to start again. you are under no obligation to be the person you were five minutes ago if you no longer feel that's the person you are. nor you want to be.

you have the right to grow.

— *becoming a sunflower*

it is a heavy thing the one that lingers on my chest when
the loss comes. the hardest goodbye. when you know
there's no possibility to rekindle a new beginning. to
make up for it. as this is the only time when there are
truly no other doors. no solutions.

we spend our lives doing and undoing mistakes but
now. this is it. i can't fix this. this is the most real and
raw thing that i ever saw and it's looking at me in the
eye. i am naked. this is unfiltered. and i can't tell if the
pain was here before waiting in a box inside my chest to
be pulled out. and it is running all over itself now your
absence has opened it.

i don't know if it was in my hands the power to save
you. and it's eating me alive that my words can't make
it past your skin now. do you hear me. these hands
would have done anything to make you stay. i would
have sewed myself to you to protect you from it in case
it came and you weren't ready to leave.

but it is so impatient. so whimsical. this fate.
so i gathered my rage and blood and used them to
write a letter.
you could have sent a sign it said.
the sky opened itself and the clouds articulated
each breath was a sign.

i wish i had known. i wish i could tell. but now it's dark
and late and these tears won't stop washing over me. do
you see me. i was not trained for this. this is acting. i am
breaking and just pulled out this facade to fool myself
but it's not working.

my pain is so selfish i can't even think of anything else rather than how i will digest it. instead of how will you be facing this journey. referring to you in past feels like drinking salt in the dryness of the desert. i can't stop thinking of how should i remember you. of what can i do for my life to be easier given the circumstances. wow. this is such a genuine moment. it is you who left and i keep making this about me.

i wonder how did it feel. did it hurt. what were your thoughts. how was your breath. did you think of what would you have done differently. questions that can't be answered always scare me the most.

i try to remember which flowers were your favorite type and curse myself for not having given them to you when your hands could still hold them. when your nose could smell the flavour of life and your fingers could feel it. it feels like you were replaced by a giant mirror and now we all can't help but see our genuine and horrifying reflection. i feel love and i'm confused. your loss has been a tsunami of several oceans and after the event i have discovered myself in waves of realization.

it takes grace to assimilate. to name. to make the present past. at peace. to get back to sleeping. to living. but fighting against it. is breaking the oath   of life. if it comes. take its hand. it can be the most devastating thing but. it is also a healing experience.

— the side effect of death

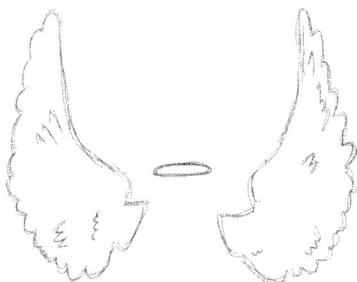

wherever you are
i hope you feel loved
accomplishing every
goal you ever set
reaching the top of
self-fulfillment
i hope you are resting
in peace softening your
inner wars. you left this place
way too soon seventeen summers are not enough
i hope they are being kind to you in heaven
cause who would have told you on
that summer morning that it would
be the last day of love
you left us wondering
how can somebody so pure
be left alone against a fate so cruel
the clouds at dawn always tell me about you
looks like today they have something
especially beautiful to say

— *letter to a lost friend*
rip anita

how to be with and without
how to miss
how to take care of my own being
how to heal an open wound
how to dance through knives

and to keep the grace and hope
in the process

— what absence taught me

some people can't help
but telling healthy ideas
in unhealthy ways

to understand
listen to their will
not their anger

— *language*

to the person who left not only her job. but her life. her
dreams. for my heart to grow in the company of love
itself. the person who sat down everyday. day after day.
week after week. and year after year. to teach me how
to be a person of grace. the person who truly sacrificed
anything needed for me to be. and taught me what is
like to speak with your heart and express with your
eyes. for healing my wounds. for kissing my scars. for
reading me at night. for waking me up in the morning
making me feel wanted. loved. needed. for giving me
peace. for understanding. for loving. for adding sugar to
my childhood and life so that it would be sweeter. for
our special connection. for giving me breath. thanks to
you i am. thanks to you i know. i am a lucky boy.

to my mother.

— you are the world

163

how can i
remain constant
think and act the same
all the time
if i'm two thirds water

— constant change lives within me

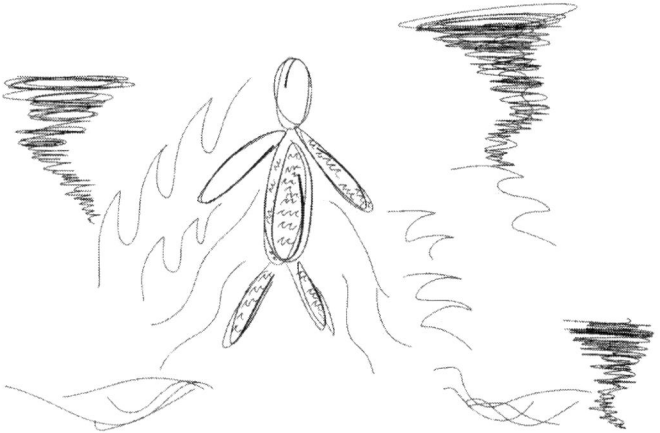

i am sorry for anytime
all the fires
happening inside of me
burned you

— letter to my family

you grab my heart in
your hands
and hold it so harshly yet
softly
you never leave me lonely
being the greatest company
standing right here
during the rough ride
life has been
from the ending till the beginning
drawing a glimpse of
light on this face
at a time i was not
sure i could ever
trust again

— *letter to self*

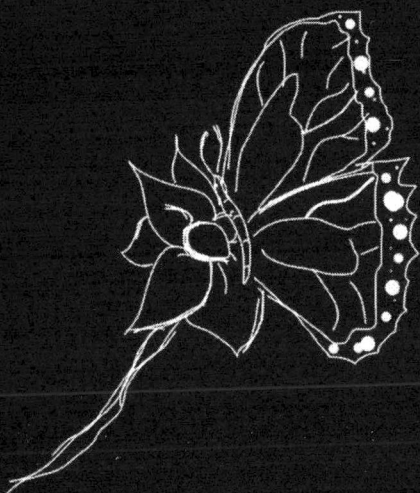

the beginning

every time you breathe
a new life is celebrating her birth
as she exhales
her way
out of your lungs

— *the beginning*

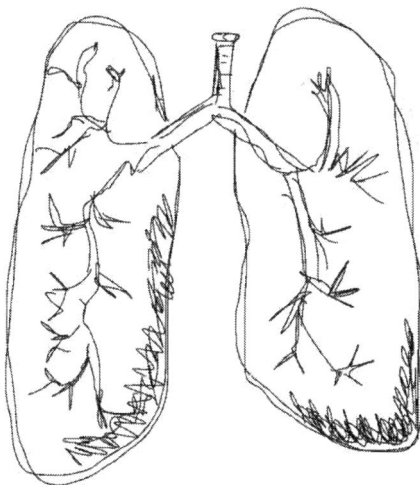

before speaking.
always ensure the person who listens
is willing to understand you.

my accent is thick
like the hair
that grows dark and strong
in every direction of my brown skin
my eyes are almond-like
the earth's color
golden brown pearls
i always get lost in the colors
of the fiercest of eagles and
i find myself back in
the tenderness of fall

— in love with my brown skin

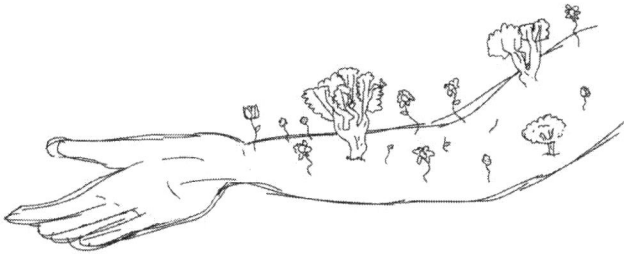

gay
is the highest compliment you can pay me

it lands at my chest in such brutal
honesty
i can't help but blooming
upon hearing it

— *offence*

i am not willing to step in an office
at 9
exit at 5
day after day
year after year
sorry not sorry
i don't like boredom
neither to work for others dreams
i'm not a machine
i rather invest my precious time
my very own way
to design my personal path
the way i like most
cause if someone has done it before
so can i

— *future planning*

let the youth dream big
sleep late and
love early
let the young people be young
daring
intense
unstable
let stability for the furniture
cause my dear
worse things than
an emotional rollescoaster
could come
let them dream big cause
ambition is not a disgrace
settling down for less than you deserve is
let them know the world is theirs
caress their wings
kiss their cheeks and
whisper to their ear
i believe in you
and watch the magic happen

— *dreamkillers*

you stand still while witnessing
with your numb eyes
the suffering of a person
whose existence
has been reduced
to a bunch of
ashes
how can
you
have the nerve
to call yourself innocent

— *entertainment*

hope is such
a diva she tends
to be so well
hidden
you can't
see her anywhere
but
she always appears if
you are willing to wait for
her entrance

you're not asked to understand
how complex sexuality can be.
that sometimes you might feel
more feminine than masculine.
that at times you might like
women then men then nobody.
that some people feel trapped in their bodies.
and so on.
perhaps you didn't need to feel so in your skin.
but others did.
respect it.
if even in the slightest of ways you don't.
i hope you have dignity enough
to remain silent and share the guilt when
those who did feel all the weight
of the complexity of sexuality
on their young. innocent backs and
needed some other backs to share some of it.
to be acknowledged. or at very the least respected.
take their lives away out of sorrow.

— *accountability*

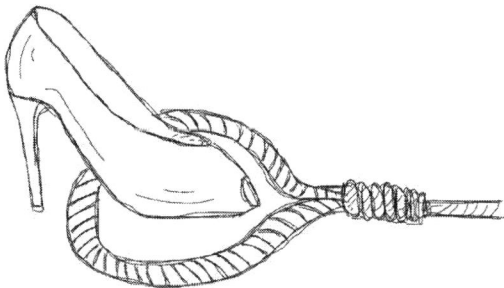

calm down sweet love.
it is my light that scares you.

i deserve to be
loved out loud

don't bother
coming at me
full of hatred
armed with empty slurs
i have blossomed now
i didn't go
from bullied
to bravery
for nothing

my right to dignity
is not up for votation

who are you
to decide what's best
for me not knowing what
to be me
feels like

— *gay people decide for gay rights. is that simple.*

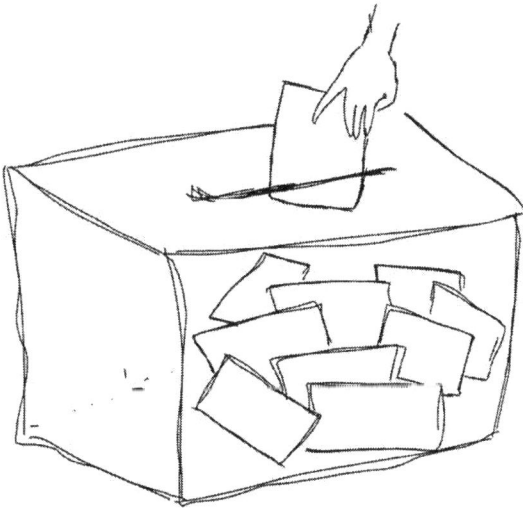

do not judge my joy as if
i can't carry the hurting
inside
while i smile
outside
just cause disgrace happened to me
doesn't force me to become one myself

the fact that i'm shattered
internally
doesn't mean i shall become a sharp blade
externally

— to be happy in hell

having the talent skill or possibility
to do something
does not
obligate me to do so
if i simply
don't want to.
i am free
to say no.
without explaining
nor excusing myself.

— i am not at your free disposal

there is
a difference
between learning
something from you and
you teaching me something

you were looking for things within me
that wouldn't come out
obedience
submission
something at your free disposal
anytime and in any way

— not your siri

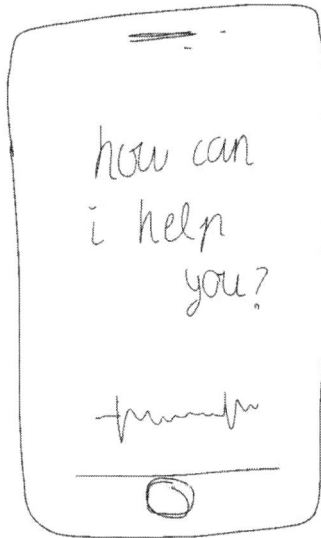

whenever people come and go
offering favours you didn't ask for
just to be rewarded
remember
you're not forced to do anything
and tell them to keep
their emotional blackmail
away from you

— *i owe you nothing*

save your tags for clothing
the to-do list
or sales season
i am not a discounted product to be sold
i am to be treated carefully
not cause i'm weak but
cause i'm complex
i am more than words can tell
more than a poem

i am a poetry collection
i am water and her cirscumtances
i change adapt destroy and heal
i am both destruction and salvation
the poison and the antidote

— i am the question to the answer

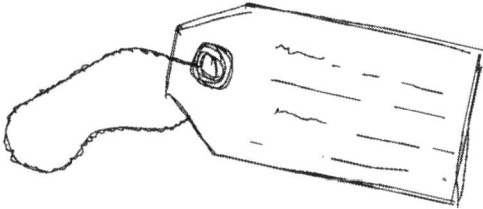

just for tonight.
place your fingers
in my bones
and dance inside of me.

you shouldn't pretend
you don't need love
nor respect
nor appreciation
as long as you love yourself
you should not mix
self-love
and basic needs

human beings are social beings
that's where our magic is

pretending to be alien to society
is not nurturing self-love
but rather neglecting your roots

— we're one

how many busy streets
full
of empty faces
have witnessed the crimes
how many lies told
how many faces have looked
somewhere else
ignoring somebody's suffering
it's not just about the bully
but the crowd
every single witness
i guess seeing me fall apart would be
some good entertainment
perhaps it made you feel powerful
at some point
to forget your own flaws
pointing out mine
but the truth is you're just
scared of yourself
and you
made me
invincible
in the process

— thank you

the magic show starts
whenever you find yourself
unwilling
to treat me right
yet expecting the best of me
wanting me close by
and attempting to make me think
you're irreplaceable.
i'll ask you to
stop for a second
and blink.
i'll be worlds away already.

— seven billion options

for what i have lived.
i could go around ripping tears
from random faces
playing feelings like a violinist.
causing the pain they caused me
back.
the abuse
the hurting
the trauma
back.
but i choose not to.
and so can you.
so don't disguise your hatred
as a product of your experiences.
the grief has taken to the surface what you
already had within.
it did not make a new you.

everything in life are stages.
as i go
from self-deceit
to recovery.
from impotence
to happiness.
from hopelessness
to peace.
from bullied
to bravery.
as i flourish.
so can you.

— i believe in you

do not wait for them to do it.
to fix your problems
to take your rights back
my dear
it doesn't work like that.
you must.
save yourself.
your rights
are not coming back by inertia.
you must be proactive.
think if you lost your car
you would look after it
fight for it. sue the thief.
now imagine that car
being your rights.
and think how paradoxical it is.
the fact that very often
people are conditioned to fight more
for what they own that
for themselves.

— *guarantee*

i know if you could
you would've crushed me
like an insect
you would've harshly pressed
my most open and painful wounds
you would've spat on me
put me down
push me off the cliff
break me
end me

but you could not

if you are not water.
i do not need you.

— *thirst | love*

i am not a musical note
moving and dancing to your melody
i have my own rythm

— *different tuning*

if somebody acts as if
it was selfish by you to
think of yourself
before you think of them
do yourself a favour
and let them go

i am a bird about to be set free
about to pluck my cage's door
calling every other caged bird
to gather in strength and
break our chains
our longing for freedom unite us
believe me is more than enough
and nothing stop us
let's rise our wings
tune our singing
if we're to be free
let it be graceful

— *revolution starts today*

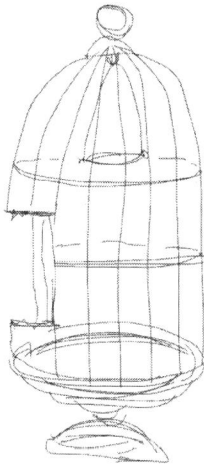

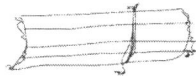

me.
asking you.
for permission.
to do or not to do
things with
my
body.

what kind of joke is that.

don't tell me to go check my sight
if i see yellow when you see pink
my dear
i aim to be free of choice
not easily agreeable
i call it the art of having an opinion
and won't even attempt
to imitate your thinking

— not your parrot

i am not
femininity or masculinity
the time spent on the gym
gay or straight
a uni degree
an education a career path
an age a number
a look a physical appearance
a decision
an impression

i am
the flavour that stays in your mouth
after a deep long and relevant
conversation with me
i am the essence
that fills in the room as i walk in
light and versatility
adaptability to change
simple and complex
a mix of
what i made out of my past and
what i make out of this moment
i can be many things
and everything that forms me
are little pieces not dependent on one other
as i am more that one thing that makes me
me

— *i am energy*

i don't want you depending on me
just as i don't want to be depending on you
i want you to be a full one
i want for us not to be two halves
but two fulls
together
trying to live our best lives
making each other company
not seizing each other
wishing each other well
regardless our own selfish wishes
loving each other genuinely
despite having multiple attractions

i want happiness for myself
and for my loved ones
keep your control
jealousy
and past traumas
away from me
as i have my own scars
to take care of

— boost my growing or go

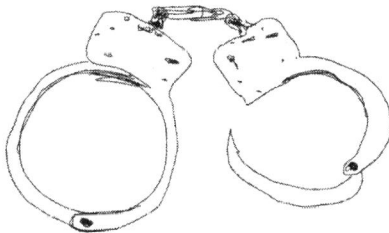

do not dare telling me
i should thank your acceptance
your respect
your indifference
do not dare insinuating
i should conform to
passive-aggressive attitudes
or degrading looks
don't take my rights for granted
don't ask me what else do i want
to be free is what i want
i crave freedom to be myself
i shall never be thankful
that my existence is respected

keeping yourself loyal towards what you are
is vital cause you can gain
a fortune or a bunch of stunning friends
but if in order to get any of that
you lost a piece of yourself
or lost yourself fully
on the way
you're losing
if conversely you loss the fortune
and the bunch of stunning friends
but you keep yourself
you're winning

— be your biggest priority

why do you keep on thinking that it's so out of context
to simply. out of nowhere. let a person know you love
them. miss them. or that you want to see them. spend
time with them. or that you like something about them.

did you ever ask yourself why are you so afraid of being
different. of looking weird in others eyes. of deviating
from the social norm. you should know saying *hello*
giving a hug or starting a conversation after a senseless
fight with a loyal friend does not make you loss your
pride—that's not what pride's for. you should know
that being kind to everyone doesn't make you stupid.
it makes you grow. it makes you smart. regardless of
other people's reaction and behavior. if you're too
obsessed about how others act upon things you'll
follow their path and not yours.

you crave things very few have but never stop to think
those who have them perhaps took a path not many
took. question things. think critically.

you always have to do whatever you believe is best
regardless of how wrong other people do you. you are
not them. teach them. but above all. teach yourself. that
you can be good despite people were not good to you.

— *normal*

your time and your energy
are your most precious gifts
choose wisely
who
you invest them in

i want someone
not to simply hold
my hand with strength
but to hold it with pride
not to let it go
in public
i want to be kissed hard
in front of the busiest station

— somebody who is proud to have you

the perfect you was here since you were born
but you have been ignoring her
trying to convince yourself
she is hidden behind those cosmetics
plastic surgeries and expensive treatments
you have isolated her
locked her up in a dark room
thinking she was not enough
the perfect you
never left
you left her
but she holds no rancor
and is willing to forgive
she is the healing
and not those creams they sell you

— *self-acceptance*

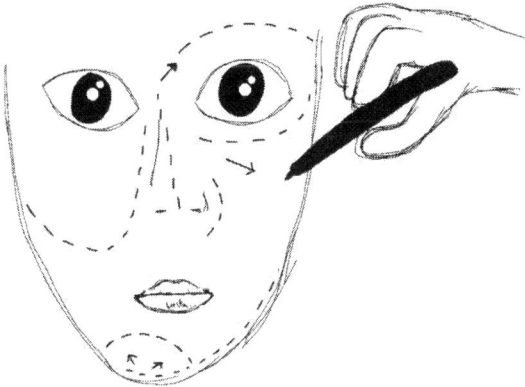

don't ever wait for somebody
to do something you want to do
anyway
because of insecurities
being with yourself
is the greatest company
you could ask for
appreciate that
nobody understands better
shares the same hobbies
enjoy the same things
aligns in thoughts
with yourself
as you do

— you are your greatest gift

being cruel is not challenging
it takes no ability nor difficulty
but remaining soft
against cruelty
harassment and
hatred
that is
at its worst
admirable

i refuse to believe
an average life awaits for me
with normal routines
and mediocre challenges
how could otherwise
this world
have put such
a remarkable weight
leaning on my back
if it wasn't
for me to be
at the very least
extraordinary

if you want to stay or leave
the door is open but
don't leave the door half
open in case
a better opportunity
shows up
i don't want rations that
come in halves
save them for yourself
till you're able to make
full ones

every feeling is alright to feel
how could somebody possibly
deny
question
or take away
your right to feel

even in this wild world
some boundaries should
never be crossed

— *the only thing that's real is what you feel*

education
is the sexiest
attribute
i could ever
ask for

i am delighted
by your existence
just your presence
makes my legs shiver

— *anatomy*

you couldn't even imagine
how many times i thought of you
coming to save me from this hell
taking me with you to an isolated place
just the two of us
how many times i fantasized of
you bursting the door down to
crush any demon that would
disturb my peace in mind

at the end i had to save myself
and who knows how things
would have ended up
if i had waited for you
to do it

why should i remain silent
if i was given a voice to express
why should i reject my feelings
if i was gifted with a heart that feels
why should i keep my hands to myself
when i was given fingers to explore
why should i remain cold
if i was given arms to hold tight
why should i stay still
if i was designed with legs to run wild

— *architecture*

you must be out
of your mind if
you expect me to
pay for your
inner frustrations
anger issues
and follow you on
your way to the
cliff

i won't jump if
you jump
i'll jump
if i want to

— *i'm noboby's dog*

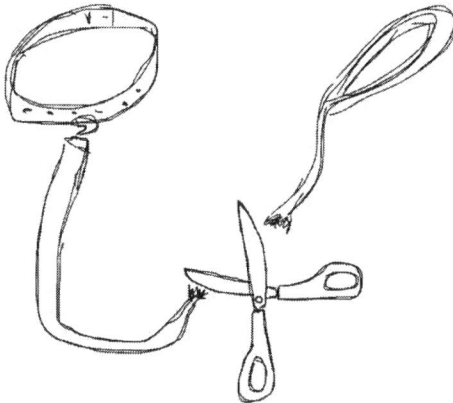

the purest peace. and the bloodiest wars.
begin from and within you.

it isn't just about the things
you do while you're out
but about the things you have missed
the journey you have carried
the person you have blossomed into
the stories you're now made of
it is about the growth

both the potential and the change
are within you but
you must stimulate them

— journey

why do you always stay in the middle
trying to please both parts
didn't they tell you
you're free to be unpleasant to some
that sometimes your intentions are irrelevant
and despite you mean no bad
your actions boost the problem
cause you're too busy trying to please everybody
you forget what you're even doing
sometimes you have to decide
where you lay and hatred will flow naturally
towards you for having an opinion
but that's part of growing

— are you helping the solution or the problem

being my partner
does not give you
a free pass to my body

— consent

you can be sober-headed and sane
impulsive and intense
calmed and nervous
clueless and perfecctionist
negative and positive
serious and goofy

you can be nothing or everything at once
don't ever let anyone
make you feel
otherwise

what goes in and out
my body
is something
only my body
can decide

— uncommon sense

be the audience to every of your poems.
trust yourself.
don't let others preferences
define the worth of your work.

— *tastes*

for me it's a way of
getting rid
of some of the weight
the pain
the sorrow
on the way
i can't define something this abstract
it's a way of translating the grief to words
of spitting some of
the sorrow i carry inside
in a bunch of pages
hoping so it lights them up and
perhaps
we can all shine together

— the reason i write

some people will hate
the meaning of you
what you're made of
what moves you
the sound of your name
will cause them rage
they will find a reason
to hate on everything
you do
they will attempt to
reduce you to ashes
to undermine your work

do not ever let
your value
your identity
in their grieving hands

— *place trust in you*

for the people who love your light when you think you've turned off. when you believe it's broken and unpure. for the people who step up and get involved with your fight. truly. after the show has concurred and the curtains come down. for the ones who support with actions and not just words. for those not scared of doing. regardless of who is watching. for those who fuel you with power. with positive energy. for those who don't make you feel pressed. not making you feel like you must explain yourself. when you don't. for those who make you feel free. safe. for those who feel like home.

— you make this heart a better one

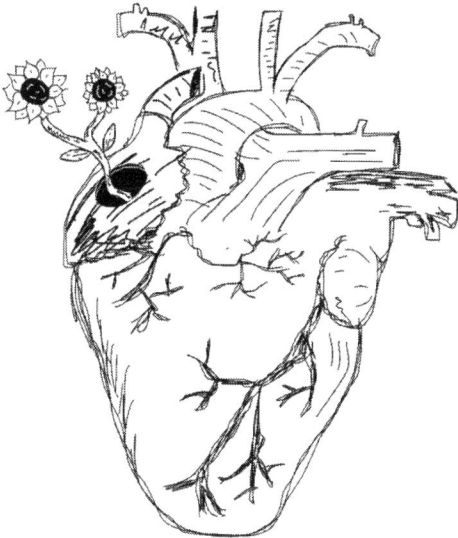

pain does no good hidden
and i want to be free
so i decided to give birth to mine
my offspring
has my blood in its pages
my baby came
from this country
i call body
from my soul opened in half

and if that helps you
in any way
have a more soft
and peaceful journey
i am willing to birth the world
over and over again

— here is to a new beginning

about the author

he was fifteen when he decided to pack his hope
and will in a bag to begin a new life in stockholm.
alberto ramos is originary from málaga spain. he left
everything behind to pursue his dream of studying
abroad while living with his bestfriend sofie and her
family. little did he know what he thought would be the
beginning was nothing but endings. his three years in
stockholm have been a journey of constant homophobic
harassment. nevertheless alberto has thick skin and is
not easily intimidated. before graduating he created
artistic projects to fight against homophobia and
bullying catching the attention of mainstream media.
since a very young age alberto has enjoyed every
form of activity that helps him to express and to
communicate. during his eighteen years of life he has
been traveling the world. learning languages. writing.
photographing. dancing. and drawing. among other
things. alberto is very passionate about his art and he
firmly believes things events and situations in life are
nothing but what we turn them to be. and here is his
attempt to make something inspiring as a product of his
painful experiences.

important information

whenever you feel the weight on your back is too much to handle. life's too rough. it isn't worth to be alive. your breath becomes so heavy you begin to think of putting an end to your life. as soon as any of those thoughts (no matter the intensity) come to your beautiful mind and you have no way to vent nor see a solution. please call.

argentina: **02234930430**   australia: **131114**

austria: **017133374**   belgium: **106**

botswana: **3911270**   brazil: **212339191**

canada: **5147234000**   croatia: **014833888**

denmark: **70201201**   egypt: **7621602**

estonia: **3726558088**   finland: **010 195 202**

france: **0145394000**   germany: **08001810771**

holland: **09000767**   hong kong: **2382 0000**

hungary: **116123**   india: **8888817666**

ireland: **8457909090**   italy: **800860022**

japan: **352869090**   mexico: **5255102550**

new zealand: **800543354**   norway: **81533300**

philippines: **28969191**   poland: **5270000**

portugal: **21 854 07 40**   russia: **0078202577577**

spain: **914590050**   south africa: **0514445691**

sweden: **317112400**   switzerland: **143**

united kingdom: **8457909090**

united states: **18002738255**

if you are homosexual. bisexual. lesbian. trans. queer.
pansexual. asexual. and more. you can text and call
here.

(+1) 1-866-488-7386

i love everything you are.

the visual journey

eighteen is not an inert product
it is a seed
a living thing
and if you're interested in its development
here's where you can watch it grow
instagram & twitter – @albeertoramos

see you soon